Presidents

John Adams

A MyReportLinks.com Book

Stephen Feinstein

MyReportLinks.com Books

an imprint of

 Enslow Publishers, Inc.
Box 398, 40 Industrial Road
Berkeley Heights, NJ 07922
USA

MyReportLinks.com Books, an imprint of Enslow Publishers, Inc. MyReportLinks®
is a registered trademark of Enslow Publishers, Inc.

Library of Congress Cataloging-in-Publication Data

Feinstein, Stephen.
John Adams : a MyReportLinks.com book / Stephen Feinstein.
     p. cm. — (Presidents)
   Includes bibliographical references and index.
   Summary: A biography of the second President of the United States, who
also served as the country's ambassador to France and as its first Vice President.
    ISBN 0-7660-5001-7
    1. Adams, John, 1735–1826—Juvenile literature. 2. Presidents—United
States—Biography—Juvenile literature. [1. Adams, John, 1735–1826. 2.
Presidents.] I. Title. II. Series.
    E322 .F45 2002
    973.4'4'092—dc21   2001004301

Printed in the United States of America

10 9 8 7 6 5 4 3 2

To Our Readers:
Through the purchase of this book, you and your library gain access to the Report Links that specifically
back up this book.
The Publisher will provide access to the Report Links that back up this book and will keep these Report
Links up to date on **www.myreportlinks.com** for three years from the book's first publication date.
We have done our best to make sure all Internet addresses in this book were active and appropriate when
we went to press. However, the author and the Publisher have no control over, and assume no
liability for, the material available on those Internet sites or on other Web sites they may link to.
The usage of the MyReportLinks.com Books Web site is subject to the terms and conditions stated on the
Usage Policy Statement on **www.myreportlinks.com**.
A password may be required to access the Report Links that back up this book. The password is found on
the bottom of page 4 of this book.
Any comments or suggestions can be sent by e-mail to comments@myreportlinks.com or to the address
on the back cover.

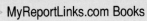
Contents

About MyReportLinks.com Books

MyReportLinks.com Books
Great Books, Great Links, Great for Research!

MyReportLinks.com Books present the information you need to learn about your report subject. In addition, they show you where to go on the Internet for more information. The pre-evaluated Report Links, listed on **www.myreportlinks.com**, save hours of research time and link to dozens—even hundreds—of Web sites, source documents, and photos related to your report topic.

To Our Readers:

Each Report Link has been reviewed by our editors, who will work hard to keep only active and appropriate Internet addresses in our books and up to date on our Web site. However, the author and the Publisher have no control over, and assume no liability for, the material available on those Internet sites, or on other Web sites they may link to.

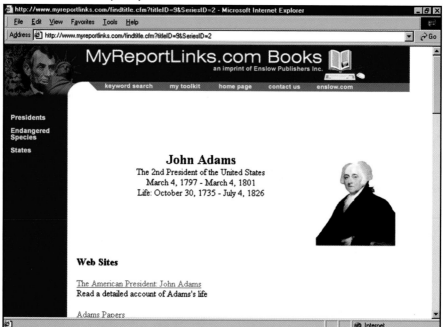

Access:

The Publisher will try to keep the Report Links that back up this book up to date on our Web site for three years from the book's first publication date. Please enter **PAD2186** if asked for a password.

Report Links

The Internet sites described below can be accessed at
http://www.myreportlinks.com

*EDITOR'S CHOICE

▶ The American President: John Adams

The American Presidency series contains a biography of John Adams.
Among other things, you will find information about Adams's family and
his life before and after the presidency.

Link to this Internet site from http://www.myreportlinks.com

*EDITOR'S CHOICE

▶ Adams Papers

From the Massachusetts Historical Society comes this collection of letters
and diaries written by members of the Adams family. These documents
chronicle America's development from the 1750s to the 1880s.

Link to this Internet site from http://www.myreportlinks.com

*EDITOR'S CHOICE

▶ John Adams: 2nd President of the United States

Presidents of the United States (POTUS) offers an overview of Adams's
life and political career and a gateway to related resources on the Internet.
You will find facts and figures on the election of 1797 and information
about the members of Adams's cabinet.

Link to this Internet site from http://www.myreportlinks.com

*EDITOR'S CHOICE

▶ LIBERTY! The American Revolution

This site discusses how the colonies gained independence from Britain
and what liberty and freedom mean today. Featured are a time line of the
Revolution, objects used in colonial America, and a game that explores the
events of the war.

Link to this Internet site from http://www.myreportlinks.com

*EDITOR'S CHOICE

▶ Objects from the Presidency

By navigating through this site you will find objects related to all the
United States presidents, including John Adams. You can also read a brief
description of the era he lived in and learn about the office of the
presidency.

Link to this Internet site from http://www.myreportlinks.com

*EDITOR'S CHOICE

▶ America's Library: The Revolutionary Period

America's Library, a site designed specifically for young adults, is part of
the Library of Congress Web site. This page describes what life was like
during the revolutionary period. You will also find links to events, such as
the Boston Massacre, and individuals, such as Abigail Adams.

Link to this Internet site from http://www.myreportlinks.com

Report Links

The Internet sites described below can be accessed at
http://www.myreportlinks.com

▶ **Abigail Adams**

This site contains Abigail Adams's biography, where you will learn about her politics on the Revolution, slavery, and women's rights through the letters she wrote. You can also test your knowledge of Abigail Adams with a brief quiz.

Link to this Internet site from http://www.myreportlinks.com

▶ **Abigail Adams Historical Society, Inc.**

Abigail Adams was not only the wife of John Adams and the mother of John Quincy, she was also very influential in politics. Abigail was a pioneer of women's rights and helped to shape John Adams's political philosophy. This site is a great place to find information on the nation's second first lady.

Link to this Internet site from http://www.myreportlinks.com

▶ **Abigail Smith Adams**

Part of the official White House series on First Ladies, this site offers a profile of Abigail Adams. Abigail Adams had a great influence on her husband's political and social thinking during his presidency.

Link to this Internet site from http://www.myreportlinks.com

▶ **Alien and Sedition Acts of the United States**

The Alien and Sedition Acts were created after the American Revolution to give the president the power to imprison foreigners suspected of activities posing a threat to the United States government. This site explains the acts and the nation's reaction to them.

Link to this Internet site from http://www.myreportlinks.com

▶ **The American Presidency: John Adams**

At this site you will find a biography of John Adams. Here you will learn about his early life and rise to the office of the presidency. You will also find a link to Adams's inaugural address, and quick facts highlighting important events in his life and administration.

Link to this Internet site from http://www.myreportlinks.com

▶ **American Presidents: Life Portraits: John Adams**

At this Web site you will find essential information about John Adams, including "Life Facts" and "Did you know?" trivia. You will also find a letter written by John Adams to Thomas Jefferson.

Link to this Internet site from http://www.myreportlinks.com

Any comments? Contact us: **comments@myreportlinks.com**

Report Links

The Internet sites described below can be accessed at http://www.myreportlinks.com

▶ **The Avalon Project at the Yale Law School: The Papers of John Adams**

Yale University's Avalon Project contains a small library of speeches and proclamations by John Adams. Included are his inaugural address, annual messages, messages to Congress, and his proclamations.

Link to this Internet site from http://www.myreportlinks.com

▶ **Boston Massacre Trials 1770**

This site contains an in-depth study of the Boston Massacre and questions whether blame should fall upon the British or Bostonians. Learn more about the events that led to the American Revolution.

Link to this Internet site from http://www.myreportlinks.com

▶ **The City of Quincy**

Quincy, Massachusetts, once called Braintree, was the home of two United States presidents, John Adams and John Quincy Adams. The town's Web site offers a tour of this historic city.

Link to this Internet site from http://www.myreportlinks.com

▶ **Declaring Independence: Drafting the Documents**

In June 1776, John Adams, Benjamin Franklin, Thomas Jefferson, Roger Sherman, and Robert R. Livingston were named to draft a declaration of independence. This site offers an account of how the document evolved from Jefferson's rough draft to the final text.

Link to this Internet site from http://www.myreportlinks.com

▶ **Documents from the Continental Congress and Constitutional Convention**

The Library of Congress Web site provides its viewers with more than two hundred documents relating to the work of the Continental Congress and the drafting of the Constitution.

Link to this Internet site from http://www.myreportlinks.com

▶ **Echoes from the White House**

At this PBS Web site you will find profiles of several United States presidents, including John Adams. Here you can take a virtual tour of the White House and learn how the White House has changed over the years.

Link to this Internet site from http://www.myreportlinks.com

 The Internet sites described below can be accessed at
http://www.myreportlinks.com

▶ **"I Do Solemnly Swear . . ."**

This site contains memorabilia from John Adams's inauguration. Read Adams's inaugural address and a letter written by George Washington to Henry Knox two days before Adams's inauguration.

Link to this Internet site from http://www.myreportlinks.com

▶ **John Adams: Ego in Retreat**

This site is dedicated to presidents thought to have had "An Independent Cast of Mind." Here you will find a brief description of John Adams's character, a historical document, and a video clip.

Link to this Internet site from http://www.myreportlinks.com

▶ **John Adams: "Thoughts on Government"**

This essay written by John Adams was originally published in pamphlet form in 1776. Adams's essay reveals his views on what government should be.

Link to this Internet site from http://www.myreportlinks.com

▶ **Mr. President: John Adams**

This brief profile of John Adams provides "fast facts" about his life, a quote, and highlights from his administration.

Link to this Internet site from http://www.myreportlinks.com

▶ **On These Walls: The John Adams Building**

This Library of Congress Web site provides a brief history of the John Adams Building. Construction was begun on the building in 1935. It was opened to the public in 1939.

Link to this Internet site from http://www.myreportlinks.com

▶ **Thomas Jefferson to John Adams**

At this Library of Congress Web site you will find a letter written by Thomas Jefferson to John Adams. In the letter, Jefferson discusses self government in Europe and Spanish America.

Link to this Internet site from http://www.myreportlinks.com

Report Links

 The Internet sites described below can be accessed at
http://www.myreportlinks.com

▶Time Line, America During the Age of Revolution

This time line of the American Revolution is a great source for learning about the laws that created tension between the American colonies and Great Britain.

Link to this Internet site from http://www.myreportlinks.com

▶White House Historical Association

At the White House Historical Association you can explore the rich history of the White House and the presidents of the United States. You can also take a virtual tour of the White House, visit the president's park, and experience past presidential inaugurations.

Link to this Internet site from http://www.myreportlinks.com

▶The White House: John Adams

Part of the official White House series on presidents, this site offers a profile of Adams and his contributions to the American struggle for independence.

Link to this Internet site from http://www.myreportlinks.com

▶*World Almanac for Kids Online:* John Adams

The *World Almanac for Kids Online* Web site explores Adams's diplomatic service, vice presidency, presidency, and retirement.

Link to this Internet site from http://www.myreportlinks.com

▶XYZ Affair

This site explains the story behind the XYZ Affair. Learn who the key players were and how relations between America and France were improved.

Link to this Internet site from http://www.myreportlinks.com

▶XYZ Correspondence

In the late 1700s, America's relationship with France became strained. France began seizing American ships. As Americans called for war, John Adams tried to resolve the situation peacefully. The attempt at negotiation became known as the XYZ Affair.

Link to this Internet site from http://www.myreportlinks.com

Highlights

1735—*Oct. 30*:* Born in Braintree, Massachusetts. Braintree is now known as Quincy.

1764—*Oct. 25:* Marries Abigail Smith in Weymouth, Massachusetts.

1770—Defends in court British soldiers accused in the Boston Massacre.

Elected to the Massachusetts legislature.

1774—Elected as delegate to the First Continental Congress.

1777—Appointed as commissioner to France.

1780–1782—As minister to the Netherlands, he obtains that country's recognition of American independence.

1783—Helps negotiate the Treaty of Paris, officially ending the Revolutionary War.

1785—Appointed minister to Great Britain.

1789—Elected first vice president of the United States, serving with President Washington.

1792—Reelected as Washington's vice president.

1796—Elected second president of the United States.

1798—Signs into law the controversial Alien and Sedition Acts.

1824—Sees his son John Quincy Adams elected president.

1826—*July 4:* Dies at home in Quincy, Massachusetts.

*According to the calendar in use in 1735, Adams's date of birth was October 19. It was not until the Georgian calendar was adopted, in 1752, that October 19 became October 30.

Chapter 1

A Sea Adventure, 1778

The Revolutionary War was raging in the American colonies. John Adams and his wife, Abigail, had a difficult decision to make. In November 1777, the Continental Congress had elected John Adams as a joint commissioner—with Benjamin Franklin and Arthur Lee—to represent his country in France. Adams would have to cross the Atlantic Ocean and join the other two men who were already there. Together they would try to obtain French support for the war.

John and Abigail Adams decided that he should accept the assignment. The decision was difficult because they were devoted to each other and to their children. If Adams accepted the assignment, he would be far away from home for a long time. Their oldest son, ten-year-old John Quincy Adams, would accompany his father to France.

Adams and his son boarded the frigate *Boston* on February 13, 1778. Because of stormy weather, the small warship was not able to set sail until February 19. That day, after the *Boston* had gone only a short distance beyond Boston Harbor, Adams saw three British ships ahead. Captain Tucker, assuming the ships to be merchant vessels, ordered his crew to approach and attack the British ships. When they came within closer range, the guns on the British ships became visible. These were warships, not merchant ships! Tucker ordered his crew to flee from the British as fast as possible. Two of the British ships were left behind, but one followed in pursuit.

The next day, thick clouds gathered and the wind increased. With the British frigate gaining on them, the Boston crew tried to set up their guns for battle. The ship was rolling and pitching so much, though, that this proved impossible. In the evening, a lieutenant advised Adams and his son to take refuge down below in their berth (the sleeping area). Sleep was impossible because of the violent motion of the ship. Suddenly a loud crash shook the vessel! Adams thought they had been hit by fire from the British guns. It turned out to be lightning. Four sailors on deck had been struck down, and one of them died soon after.

Meanwhile, it was discovered that the mainmast had been damaged. Then, a voice cried out that the powder room was open. Small casks of gunpowder were scattered about. If lightning were to strike the powder, Adams knew that the ship could be blown to bits. The crew scrambled to secure the powder, averting a disaster.

By dawn, the enemy ship was nowhere in sight. Adams had escaped one danger, but found another looming. For the next three days and nights, the ship struggled through a powerful hurricane. In Adams's words, "The wind blowing against the current, not directly, but in various angles, produced a tumbling sea, vast mountains of water above us, and as deep caverns below us, the mountains sometimes dashing against each other . . . not unfrequently breaking on the ship, threatened to bury us all at once in the deep."[1]

During the storm, Adams wondered if it had been a good idea to bring his son along on such a dangerous voyage. But the young John Quincy proved to be a brave boy. Adams was proud of him. He wrote, "The child's behaviour gave me a satisfaction, that I cannot express. Fully sensible of our danger, he was constantly endeavouring to bear up under it with a manly courage and patience."[2]

On March 10, the *Boston* captured a British merchant ship called the *Martha*. The elder Adams took part in the fighting, along with the crew. Captain Tucker later commended him for his bravery. When he asked Adams why he had volunteered to help, Adams replied that he felt he ought to do his share of the fighting.

On April 1, about six weeks after leaving Boston Harbor, the *Boston* arrived safely in Bordeaux, France. John Adams, the man who would one day become the second president of the United States, went ashore with his son, John Quincy, a future president himself.

Chapter 2

Early Years, 1735–1758

John Adams, the first child of John and Susanna Boylston Adams, was born on October 30, 1735, at the family homestead in the town of Braintree (later renamed Quincy) in the colony of Massachusetts. The home was a typical New England house, known as a "saltbox." John's parents were well-respected members of the community. His father, a farmer and church deacon, was descended from the Puritans who had founded the Massachusetts colony in the 1600s. John's mother came from a leading family of Boston-area merchants and physicians.

John grew up in a Puritan household. The family attended church every Sunday. The Puritans believed in a very strict form of Christianity and in a life of simplicity and hard work. They had come to America to escape religious persecution in England. Once established in the colonies, however, Puritans showed little tolerance for other religious ideas or ways of life. Interestingly, John would later reject narrow views of religion when choosing to become a lawyer.

John was a bright young boy. Because his father had already taught him to read, John was far ahead of his classmates once he began attending Mrs. Belcher's one-room schoolhouse. Mrs. Belcher taught reading, writing, and arithmetic. John and his classmates had to read aloud, in unison, passages from the Puritan textbook *The New England Primer*. It contained the alphabet, the Lord's Prayer, the Roman numerals, the Ten Commandments, a catechism, and bits of moral instruction. John soon became bored with his reading lessons. As for arithmetic, John took the book home and quickly taught himself all the lessons. Once again, he was far ahead of the other students.

Hard at Play

Now that school had become a place of boredom, John's attention turned more and more toward the outdoors. He constantly devised ways to avoid school. Alone or with his friends and two younger brothers, Peter and Elihu, John would spend much of his time roaming around the countryside. In the winter, the boys enjoyed going ice skating on the frozen ponds. In the summer, they spent many

Encyclopedia Americana: John Adams - Microsoft Internet Explorer

File Edit View Go Favorites Help

Address http://gi.grolier.com/presidents/ea/bios/02pjohn.html   Links

The American Presidency

| Inaugural Address | Quick Facts | The Presidents | EA Contents |

John Adams

National Archives
JOHN ADAMS
Biography

John Adams, ad'[sch]mz, 2d PRESIDENT OF THE UNITED STATES. He devoted his life to politics, participating with distinction first in the revolutionary activities of Boston and Philadelphia and later in the founding of the republic. He served as a Massachusetts delegate to the Continental

http://gi.grolier.com/presidents/preshome.html   Internet zone

▲ *John Adams, the second U.S. president, was born into a family whose ancestors founded the Plymouth colony, in the 1600s.*

carefree hours swimming, sailing toy boats, and flying kites. John's favorite activity, though, was hunting. By the time he was ten, he had learned to use a gun, and as soon as school let out, he would head for the woods to hunt deer, squirrel, partridge, and grouse.

John's father became concerned about his son's lack of interest in school. John's boredom became even more obvious once he began attending Mr. Joseph Cleverly's Latin school. John especially disliked Cleverly because the man scolded him and would not allow him to progress at his own rapid rate. At that point in his life, John considered school to be a total waste of time.

Deacon Adams wanted his son to attend college and become a minister. He was aware that John was very bright, but it seemed as if the boy was interested only in hunting and was wasting his intellectual gifts. When Deacon Adams asked his son what he wanted to be when he grew up, John replied that he wanted to be a farmer. Deacon Adams, deter-mined to put some sense into the boy, said, "I will show you what it is to be a farmer. You shall go with me to Penn Ferry tomorrow morning and help me get thatch."[1] So father and son spent all of the next day along the creek, knee-deep in mud, bending, cutting, and tying thick bundles of straw. They came home in the evening with sore muscles, exhausted and caked in mud. When Deacon Adams asked John if he would still be satisfied being a farmer, the boy answered, "Yes, sir, I like it very well." His exhausted father responded, "Aye, but I don't like it so well, so you shall go to school."[2]

Unfortunately, the farming lesson had not swayed young John. By the time John was fourteen, Deacon Adams worried that his son would not be ready to go to college when the time came. When John complained about his Latin teacher and asked if he could instead study with Joseph Marsh, Deacon Adams agreed. He went the next day to speak to Marsh and arranged for his son to study with him. Surprisingly, John liked Marsh, a true scholar, and took to his studies with enthusiasm.

 ## Harvard Man

In 1751, at age sixteen, John was admitted to Harvard College in Cambridge, Massachusetts. His studies with Marsh had prepared him to pass the entrance exam. John's father had to sell ten acres of land to pay for his son's college tuition and board.

John's educational horizons were broadened during his four years at Harvard. Even in an atmosphere of strict discipline and an emphasis on religious studies, he developed a love of learning. In addition to religion, John studied Latin and Greek, mathematics, logic, and science. He still believed in the teachings of the Bible, but the narrow views of the Puritan church no longer appealed to him.

In 1755, John Adams graduated from Harvard near the top of his class with a bachelor of arts degree. He was immediately offered a job as schoolmaster of a new one-room schoolhouse in Worcester, Massachusetts. Unfortunately, Adams did not enjoy teaching. Against his parents' objections, he began to consider a career as a trial lawyer.

A year after starting the teaching job, Adams began to study law under James Putnam, a successful Worcester lawyer. For the next two years, he lived at Putnam's house. He continued to teach school during the day. In the evenings he prepared legal briefs and discussed court cases with Putnam. In 1759, Adams was admitted to the Massachusetts bar (the state's association of lawyers and other legal professionals) and began practicing law.

Back Forward Stop Review Home Explore Favorites History

Chapter 3 ▶

Lawyer and Revolutionary, 1758–1777

In 1758, John Adams moved back to his hometown of Braintree and set up a law office in his family's home. Finding clients was a struggle during the first few years. Clients usually found Adams by word of mouth. He spent time talking about his work to the well-connected members of the community. He also visited neighboring towns and introduced himself to people such as judges and sheriffs who could direct him to potential clients. He continued to study law in his spare time.

Often Adams would travel twelve miles each way on horseback to observe court proceedings in Boston. Among the lawyers he met were James Otis and Jeremiah Gridley. They became mentors to Adams. Eventually, with Otis's help, Adams opened a law office in Boston and spent more and more of his time there.

▶ "Child Independence"

In 1761, Adams observed a trial that was to leave a deep impression on him. It had to do with whether Britain's Parliament had the right to make laws for the colonies. Parliament had ordered the Massachusetts court to allow customs officials to search any colonist's home or place of business for smuggled goods. A growing number of colonists had taken to smuggling to avoid paying the new taxes Britain had imposed on trade. The British were looking to raise money to pay for their war with the French, known as the French and Indian War, which was winding down.

James Otis argued on behalf of the colonists opposed to Britain's policy. Jeremiah Gridley argued on behalf of Parliament. Although Otis argued brilliantly, the British won the case. The trial influenced public opinion and showed a division in the loyalties of the American colonists. This division would steadily grow wider in the coming years. After the trial, Adams wrote, "Then and there, the child Independence was born!"[1]

In that same year, on May 25, Adams's father died during an influenza epidemic. Adams inherited farmland

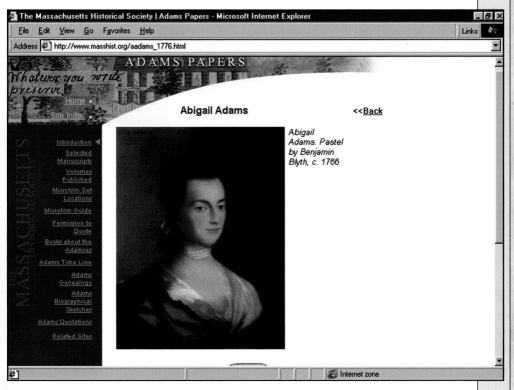

This 1766 portrait of Abigail Adams was painted not long after she married John Adams. A woman of great strength and intellect, she ran their farm, cared for their children, and managed their finances during her husband's many diplomatic trips overseas. John Adams sought her advice throughout his life.

and a small house next to the home in which he was born. Now that he owned land and was finding success in his law practice, Adams decided it was time to get married.

Adams and Abigail Smith

As a young man, Adams had had romantic feelings for a young woman named Hannah Quincy, but at the time he had not been ready for marriage. Any other sort of relationship was unthinkable for the puritanical Adams. Now, he turned his attention to seventeen-year-old Abigail Smith of Weymouth, Massachusetts. Adams had met her four years earlier. After a six-month courtship, Adams asked Abigail's father, the Reverend William Smith, for his daughter's hand in marriage. Elizabeth Quincy Smith, Abigail's mother, had hoped for a wealthier suitor. She asked for a delay, hoping to change her daughter's mind. Abigail's mind would not be changed, though it was not until three years later, on October 25, 1764, that John Adams and Abigail Smith were married.

The newlyweds set up house on the farm in Braintree that Adams had inherited. Adams divided his time between legal work and farming. Abigail, a highly intelligent and well-read young woman with an aptitude for mathematics, helped run the farm and manage the family's finances. The young couple was very happy, and before long, their family grew to include children—first Abigail "Nabby" Amelia; then John Quincy; Susanna, who died in infancy; Charles; and Thomas Boylston. Whenever Adams was away on business for extended periods, he and Abigail exchanged letters. They continued to write letters to each other for the fifty-four years of their marriage.

Tools   Search   Notes   Discuss   Go!

The Stamp Act

Throughout the 1760s, tensions continued to build between Britain and the American colonies. In 1763, Britain and France signed a peace treaty that finally ended the French and Indian War. The British were now determined to tax the American colonists to pay for that war. In 1765, the British Parliament passed the Stamp Act, which required the colonists to pay a tax on imported goods. The colonists were outraged. John Adams's cousin, Samuel Adams, organized a radical group of Bostonians called the Sons of Liberty to protest British policies.

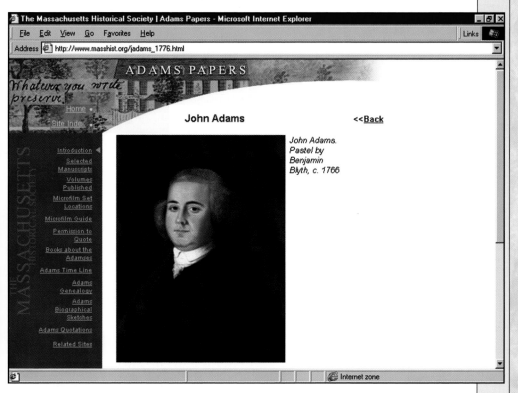

This portrait of John Adams captures him as he looked in 1766, when he was engaged in protests against British policies in the American colonies.

The Series   Presidential History Resources   Election 2000   "The War Room" Game   Student Magazine

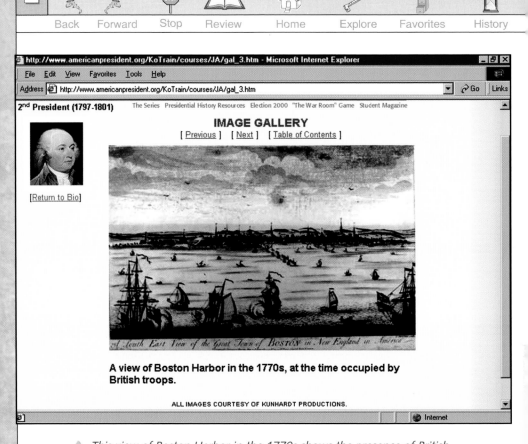

IMAGE GALLERY
[Previous]   [Next]   [Table of Contents]

[Return to Bio]

A view of Boston Harbor in the 1770s, at the time occupied by British troops.

ALL IMAGES COURTESY OF KUNHARDT PRODUCTIONS.

This view of Boston Harbor in the 1770s shows the presence of British ships. By the late 1760s, John Adams had moved his family from their farm in Braintree to Boston as his law practice became more successful.

John Adams, also angry at high-handed, oppressive British policies, engaged in his own protest in the form of letters to the *Boston Gazette*. In his letters to the newspaper, Adams argued that Parliament had no right to tax the colonies. He also made that argument, along with James Otis and Jeremiah Gridley, before representatives of the British government. By this time, colonists were boycotting British goods, and British merchants were complaining about the loss of business. Finally, Britain repealed the Stamp Act.

In 1767, Britain again attempted to raise tax money in the colonies by means of the Townshend Acts. New taxes brought forth renewed protests from the colonists. In that climate of unrest, Adams's law practice thrived. In 1768, he successfully defended John Hancock in court against the charge of smuggling wine into Boston without paying the required tax. The trial helped Adams gain widespread admiration among American patriots, those colonists who opposed British policies. He was spending so much of his time in Boston that he and Abigail decided to move the family there.

Boston Massacre

Relations between Britain and the colonies continued to deteriorate. The colonists engaged in protests and boycotts

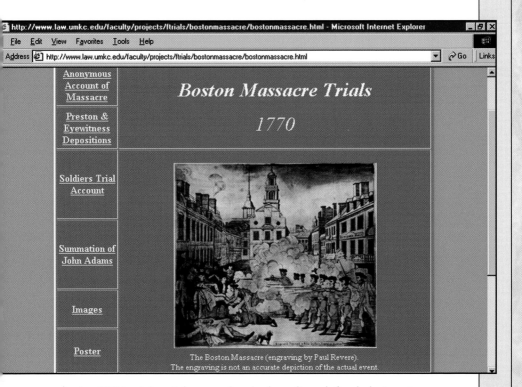

In 1770, John Adams, who had earlier defended American patriots, agreed to defend the eight British soldiers involved in the Boston Massacre.

of British goods. Britain responded by sending thousands of troops into Boston. It was only a matter of time until tragedy struck. On March 5, 1770, a group of British soldiers fired into a crowd of defiant Bostonians, killing five patriots and wounding several others.

Adams, although sympathetic to the patriots, felt that every man had the right to a lawyer. He agreed to defend the eight British soldiers charged in what became known as the Boston Massacre. Adams by this time was widely regarded as a brilliant lawyer. But his successful defense of the British soldiers proved highly unpopular. For a time it threatened to ruin his law practice. Adams moved his family back to Braintree, where Abigail could again manage the farm.

▷ Boston Tea Party

Adams continued to write in support of the colonists' resistance to the British. "No taxation without representation" was a key theme. It referred to the belief that the British Parliament had no right to tax the colonists, because the colonies were not represented in Parliament. For the next several years, Adams served as a member of the Massachusetts legislature. In 1773, patriots disguised as American Indians crept aboard British ships in Boston Harbor and dumped 342 chests of tea overboard. Their act was in response to taxes that remained on British tea exported to the colonies. Adams approved of this act, which became known as the Boston Tea Party. Britain reacted by passing further restrictive measures known as the Intolerable Acts. In the spring of 1774, Britain closed off Boston Harbor to all shipping and sent thousands more troops into the city.

▷ First Continental Congress

That year, the colonists decided to organize politically in order to resist British policies. Each colony elected

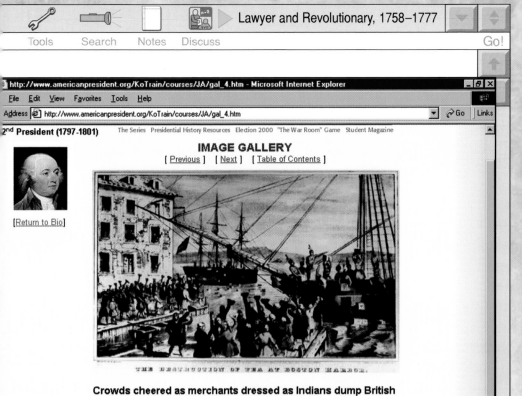

2nd President (1797-1801)   The Series Presidential History Resources Election 2000 "The War Room" Game Student Magazine

IMAGE GALLERY
[Previous]   [Next]   [Table of Contents]

[Return to Bio]

THE DESTRUCTION OF TEA AT BOSTON HARBOR.

Crowds cheered as merchants dressed as Indians dump British tea into Boston Harbor in the "Boston Tea Party" in 1773.

ALL IMAGES COURTESY OF KUNHARDT PRODUCTIONS.

Internet

In 1773, patriots dressed as American Indians dumped chests of tea into Boston Harbor as a protest against taxes levied on tea shipped to the colonies.

delegates to meet in Philadelphia for the First Continental Congress. Adams was elected as a Massachusetts delegate, along with his cousin Samuel Adams and three other men. The Congress began on September 5, 1774. Adams met delegates from the other colonies, including George Washington from Virginia. The delegates agreed to ban British goods in all the colonies. They drew up a petition to King George III, asserting the colonists' rights. They agreed to meet again the following year.

George III responded to the colonists' demands by sending more troops. Meanwhile, the American patriots organized a militia known as "minutemen," so-named

because they would be ready to march at a moment's notice. Compromise seemed increasingly unlikely. This drift toward war, once begun, became unstoppable. On April 19, 1775, in Lexington, Massachusetts, British troops fired what came to be known as the "shot heard round the world" as they battled a group of minutemen. Eight of the patriots were killed, and the Revolutionary War had begun.

In May 1775, Adams attended the Second Continental Congress in Philadelphia. Now that fighting had broken out between the American colonists and the British, the delegates agreed on the necessity of organizing an army to defend the colonies. The delegates agreed to

John Adams served on the committee of the Continental Congress that was charged with writing a declaration of independence. It was Adams who chose Thomas Jefferson to draft the document.

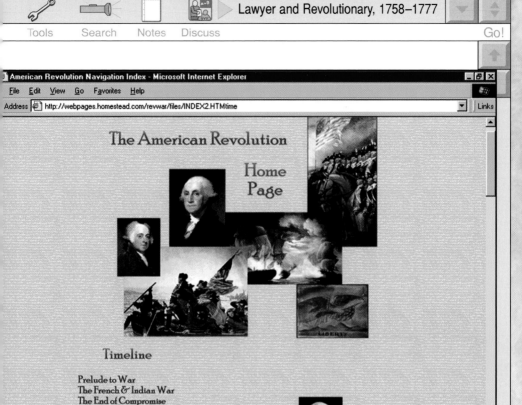

The American Revolution

Home Page

Timeline

Prelude to War
The French & Indian War
The End of Compromise
The Stamp Act
The Townshend Acts

▲ For much of the American Revolution, John Adams served his country abroad, in diplomatic missions for the struggling new nation.

Adams's proposal that George Washington, a delegate from Virginia with military experience, be made commander-in-chief of the Continental Army.

▷ Declaration

In 1776, the Continental Congress agreed on separation from Britain. A committee consisting of John Adams, Thomas Jefferson, Benjamin Franklin, Robert R. Livingston, and Roger Sherman chose Jefferson to write a declaration of independence. The Declaration was adopted on July 4, 1776. John Hancock, the man Adams had successfully defended in court in 1768, was the first to sign.

Chapter 4 ▶

Diplomat and Vice President, 1777–1797

In November 1777, the Continental Congress appointed John Adams to represent American interests in France. There he would join Benjamin Franklin and Arthur Lee, the other members of a joint American commission. Their task would be to seek French recognition of the new American nation, along with much-needed military and economic aid.

When they got to Paris, Adams and his son John Quincy stayed in the same house as Franklin and Lee. John Quincy was enrolled at a local boarding school, along with Franklin's grandson, Benjamin Bache. Right from the start, Adams was put off by the lavish lifestyle of his fellow Americans. Franklin and Lee seemed to enjoy the high society of Paris, expensive pleasures that irritated the puritanical Adams. Adams noticed that they had not kept careful records of their diplomatic activities nor did they keep account of their expenses. Nevertheless, they had managed to conclude a treaty of alliance with the French long before Adams arrived in Paris. France had already begun supplying military aid to America.

Adams brought order to the activities of the commission. But he was unable to win French recognition of the new American nation. He was growing frustrated at not making any further diplomatic progress at the French court at Versailles.

Also weighing on him was the knowledge, from his wife's many letters, that Abigail found their separation unbearable. For example, in a letter from December 1778, she wrote, "How lonely are my days. How solitary are my nights. Secluded from all society but my two little boys, and my domesticks, by the mountains of snow which surround me I could almost fancy myself in Greenland."[1]

Homeward Bound

Adams wrote Congress to recommend that one American representative in Paris would be quite enough. Congress obliged Adams by recalling him and naming Franklin the sole representative. In May 1779, Adams and his son sailed for Boston aboard the *Sensible*. Back home again, Adams

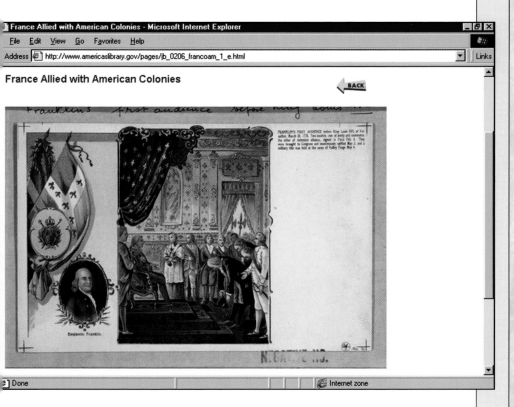

France Allied with American Colonies - Microsoft Internet Explorer

File Edit View Go Favorites Help

Address http://www.americaslibrary.gov/pages/jb_0206_francoam_1_e.html | Links

France Allied with American Colonies

BACK

Done | Internet zone

▲ *In 1777, Adams was sent to France by the Continental Congress to join Benjamin Franklin and Arthur Lee in seeking French recognition of the United States.*

served as a delegate to the Massachusetts Constitutional Convention, where he wrote the state constitution. Then, in September of that year, Adams was elected by Congress to return to Paris to negotiate a peace treaty with Britain.

On November 14, 1779, Adams boarded the *Sensible* again, this time accompanied by his nine-year-old son, Charles, and John Quincy, now twelve. Once more, Adams found the slow pace of diplomacy to be frustrating. He spent much of his spare time writing articles about America—which were translated and published in a Paris newspaper—and countless letters to Congress, friends, and Abigail.

In 1780, Adams was appointed minister to the Netherlands. He moved to Amsterdam and enrolled Charles and John Quincy in the Latin School there. Due to Adams's efforts over the next two years, the Netherlands became the first country to give diplomatic recognition to an independent America. He also arranged substantial loans for the American government from Dutch banks, which greatly helped the war effort. In October 1782, Adams returned to France to help Franklin and John Jay conclude a peace treaty with the British, who had signaled a willingness to negotiate.

▶ Treaty of Paris

On September 3, 1783, the American and British negotiators signed the Treaty of Paris, ratified on Jan. 14, 1784, formally ending the Revolutionary War. Adams went next to England and then back to the Netherlands, to negotiate another loan. In October, he wrote Abigail, asking her to come to Europe with their daughter. Adams's two younger sons, Charles and Thomas, were still enrolled in school. On June 20, 1784, Abigail and Nabby set sail from Boston on the *Active*. The ocean voyage was a rough one. Abigail wrote, "Our sickness continued for ten days, with some intermissions. We crawled upon deck whenever we were able; but it was so cold and damp, that we could not remain long upon it."[2]

John and Abigail had a joyous reunion in London on August 7, 1784, after having been apart for more than four years. They soon left for Paris, where Adams carried out trade negotiations, while Abigail and Nabby enjoyed French culture and fashion. Thomas Jefferson was now the American minister at the French court, replacing Benjamin Franklin. Adams and Jefferson, who had become friends ten years earlier in Philadelphia, resumed their close friendship.

▶ Ambassador to Great Britain

On February 24, 1785, Adams was appointed the first American ambassador to Great Britain. Although Adams had been hoping for this post, he feared that his work would be extremely difficult. His main diplomatic objective would be to improve relations between Britain and the United States. But there were many obstacles. A number of provisions in the Treaty of Paris had yet to be carried out. British troops still remained in some places on American soil. British trade policies were still restrictive. And there were still unresolved territorial disputes. Adams was well aware that America, whose economy was in shambles as a result of the war, was in a weak negotiating position.

In May 1785, the Adamses left Paris for London. For the next couple of years, they enjoyed the social life of the British city. Jefferson also came to visit on occasion, and he was always treated as a member of the Adams family. On one such visit in 1786, Adams and Jefferson toured the English countryside. At other times, they collaborated on

▲ This dwelling in Braintree (now Quincy), known as the "Old House," was purchased by John Adams in 1787. He and Abigail and their family moved in shortly afterward. It was to be the home of four generations of the Adams family. It is now part of the Adams National Historic Site.

matters of diplomacy. Adams eventually grew frustrated again with his diplomatic efforts. Believing he had accomplished little, he requested that Congress recall him, effective February 1788.

▶ Back to Braintree

On June 17, 1788, the Adamses sailed into Boston Harbor aboard the *Lucretia*. They returned to their farm in Braintree. Adams announced that he would refuse further public office. After such a long absence from home, he was happy to attend to farm matters and catch up on his reading. He needed time to observe and think about the latest political developments. However, the nation would not allow him to remain outside of politics for long.

In 1787, while Adams had been working in Europe, James Madison of Virginia and other delegates at the Constitutional Convention in Philadelphia had drawn up a constitution for the new nation. It called for a separation of power into three branches of government—executive, legislative, and judicial. This idea was a key feature of the constitution Adams had earlier written for the state of Massachusetts. The executive branch was to be headed by a president elected to a four-year term of office.

Vice President

In 1789, electors from each state chose George Washington to be the first president of the United States. Washington had emerged a hero from the Revolutionary War and was now the most popular leader in the nation. Adams, a well-regarded political figure, was also included on the ballot, but ran a distant second. Adams agreed to accept the vice-presidency. On April 30, 1789, Washington was inaugurated in New York City as America's first president. Adams became the nation's first vice president. The Adamses had to move once again, this time to New York, the original capital of the United States.

At first, Adams was quite happy in New York. There he was reunited with Thomas Jefferson, who had been appointed secretary of state in Washington's administration. Adams looked forward to working closely with his old friend.

Adams, energetic and ambitious as ever, had hoped to become president. Although he accepted the lesser political role, he still hoped to accomplish important deeds. Unfortunately, his years as vice president would prove to be extremely frustrating. Although Washington asked Adams for his opinions, he did not usually include him

when making decisions on important matters. Adams's main job was to preside over the Senate and vote only on issues where the votes were tied, to break the tie.

In the early days of Washington's first term, Adams became involved in the debate over how to address the president. Adams favored a title such as "His Electoral Highness," but this reminded people of the British regard for a monarch. Most senators scoffed at such titles, and some took to calling Adams "His Rotundity,"[3] making fun of Adams's shape, which was decidedly round.

Adams soon became resigned to what he considered to be his relatively unimportant political role. He wrote to Abigail about the vice presidency, "My country has in its wisdom contrived for me the most insignificant office that ever the invention of man contrived or his imagination conceived."[4]

▷ Two-Party System

Adding to Adams's unhappiness was the political rift that was widening between him and his friend Jefferson. During Washington's first administration, two political groups formed. The Federalists, followers of Secretary of the Treasury Alexander Hamilton, favored the interests of wealthy Northern financiers and industrialists. The Republicans, on the other hand, supported the interests of Southern property owners, farmers, and craftsmen. Adams became a Federalist, while Jefferson was sympathic to and was supported by the Republicans. Washington tried to maintain a balance between both groups when deciding on policy, but he in fact tended to favor the Federalists.

In 1790, the Adamses moved to Philadelphia, which had been chosen as the nation's temporary capital, while the brand-new capital of Washington, the District of

Columbia, or "Washington, D.C.," was being built. When George Washington was elected in 1792 for a second term as president, Adams was reelected vice president. As such, he faithfully supported all of Washington's major policies, including the controversial Jay Treaty of 1794.

When war had broken out between Britain and France in 1793, Hamilton favored the British while Jefferson, no longer a member of Washington's cabinet, favored the French. Washington, however, followed a policy of neutrality. Britain, though, had ignored American neutrality and seized American ships. The Jay Treaty was supposed to ensure British respect for American neutrality. Still, Jefferson and the Republicans were harshly critical of the treaty, seeing it as a surrender to British terms.

Some feared another war with Britain would follow. Amidst the turmoil, Washington decided not to seek a third term in office. Thus, in the election of 1796, after serving two terms as vice president, John Adams was elected as the second president of the United States. He won by a narrow electoral majority (71–68 votes) over Jefferson, who became the vice president. Back then, the person that finished second in the presidential election automatically became vice president. The system did not change until the election of 1804.

Chapter 5

America's Second President, 1797–1801

On March 4, 1797, John Adams was inaugurated as the second president of the United States. He took the oath of office at Congress Hall in Philadelphia. Abigail was unable to attend the inauguration. She stayed behind in Braintree to nurse Adams's mother, who was ill.

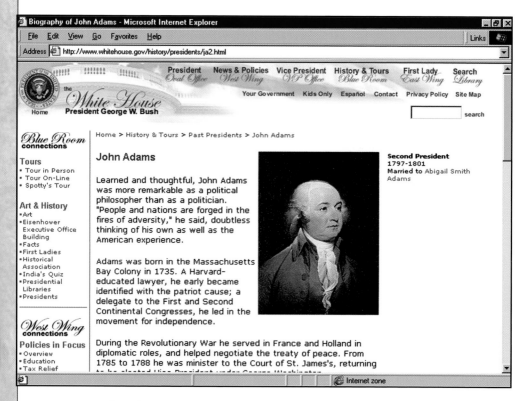

Biography of John Adams - Microsoft Internet Explorer

File   Edit   View   Go   Favorites   Help   Links

Address http://www.whitehouse.gov/history/presidents/ja2.html

President   News & Policies   Vice President   History & Tours   First Lady   Search
Oval Office West Wing   VP Office   Blue Room   East Wing   Library

the White House   Your Government   Kids Only   Español   Contact   Privacy Policy   Site Map

Home   President George W. Bush   search

Blue Room connections

Tours
• Tour in Person
• Tour On-Line
• Spotty's Tour

Art & History
• Art
• Eisenhower Executive Office Building
• Facts
• First Ladies
• Historical Association
• India's Quiz
• Presidential Libraries
• Presidents

West Wing connections

Policies in Focus
• Overview
• Education
• Tax Relief

Home > History & Tours > Past Presidents > John Adams

John Adams

Learned and thoughtful, John Adams was more remarkable as a political philosopher than as a politician. "People and nations are forged in the fires of adversity," he said, doubtless thinking of his own as well as the American experience.

Adams was born in the Massachusetts Bay Colony in 1735. A Harvard-educated lawyer, he early became identified with the patriot cause; a delegate to the First and Second Continental Congresses, he led in the movement for independence.

During the Revolutionary War he served in France and Holland in diplomatic roles, and helped negotiate the treaty of peace. From 1785 to 1788 he was minister to the Court of St. James's, returning

Second President
1797-1801
Married to Abigail Smith Adams

Internet zone

▲ John Adams—patriot, diplomat, and founding father—was inaugurated the second president of the United States on March 4, 1797.

Hoping to avoid the bitter partisan bickering that had occurred during Washington's second administration, Adams wanted to include Jefferson in his cabinet. Adams hoped the vice president's involvement would lead to a solid bipartisan approach to foreign policy decisions. However, Jefferson, wishing to maintain a degree of political independence, refused to participate. Adams's hopes of peace and harmony between the Federalists and the Republicans were doomed from the start of his administration. So was the personal friendship between Adams and Jefferson.

Britain and France were still at war, and Adams hoped to continue Washington's policy of American neutrality. This became increasingly difficult. The signing of the Jay Treaty between the United States and Britain had angered the French, because the treaty allowed British ships to continue to confiscate French cargo on American ships. So the French began seizing American ships. Three hundred American ships had been taken by the time Adams was inaugurated.

President John Adams is seen at his writing desk in this 1798 painting by William Winstanley.

▷ XYZ Affair

In October 1798, Adams sent Charles Cotesworth Pinckney and two other envoys to France to negotiate an end to the French seizures. Before the French foreign minister Charles-Maurice de Talleyrand-Périgord would agree to negotiate, three of his agents had demanded payment of $250,000, followed by a loan of $10 million from the Americans. If America refused to pay, the French threatened to declare war.

Pinckney, totally outraged, cried, "No! No! Not a sixpence!"[1] When Adams learned of the attempted bribery by the French, he told Congress that America must prepare for war with France. The three French agents were referred to as X, Y, and Z. When Americans read about the "XYZ Affair" in their newspapers, they were incensed. The nation rallied behind the Federalist slogan "Millions for defense, but not one cent for tribute."[2] Federalists in Congress demanded an outright declaration of war. Even Republicans, who previously had favored the French against the British, were ready to join Britain in its war against France.

Now that America faced a new enemy, Adams's popularity skyrocketed. Congress did indeed appropriate millions of dollars for defense. Plans were drawn up for a large military buildup and a new United States Navy. Adams appointed George Washington as commander of a thirty-thousand-man army, with Alexander Hamilton as second in command. There was only one problem—and it was a big problem. Adams knew America was in no way prepared for all-out war with France. The new nation was much too weak, militarily and economically, to withstand a possible French invasion.

So Adams chose a different course, one that would please nobody and cause his popularity to sink. It ensured that he would be a one-term president. Adams had never

△ The XYZ Affair is the subject of this engraving. The five-headed monster represents the Directory, which ruled France at the time. President Adams had sent American negotiators to France to end the seizure of American ships. The three French agents who asked the Americans for a bribe in return for an end to the seizures were referred to as X, Y, and Z.

shrunk from unpopular courses of action, as he had proved by his earlier legal defense of the British soldiers involved in the Boston Massacre. Aware that calling for a declaration of war might lead to disaster, he opted instead for an "undeclared" war. American naval vessels were authorized to seize French ships. The undeclared conflict, or Quasi-War, as it became known, would last for two-and-a-half years. During that time, America would capture eighty French ships in the West Indies while losing only one.

Shortly after the Quasi-War began, Adams, giving in to pressure from Federalists, signed into law the Alien and Sedition Acts. The purpose of the Sedition Act was to silence Republican critics of Federalist policies. Many pro-Republican newspaper editors and others were

arrested and sentenced to jail terms. Republicans, not surprisingly, were harshly critical of the Sedition Act. Jefferson anonymously wrote the *Kentucky Resolutions*, calling the Alien and Sedition Acts unconstitutional.

The Alien Acts, of which there were three, permitted Adams to round up and imprison or deport anybody considered to be an enemy alien. Although this section of the Alien Acts was never enforced, it caused hundreds of foreign residents to flee the country. Some people were tried under the Sedition Acts for criticizing the government.

Adams came under increasing attack by Federalists, as well as Republicans, because of his Quasi-War. Alexander Hamilton was angry at Adams's refusal to declare war. So were other members of Adams's cabinet, including Secretary of State Timothy Pickering, who regarded Hamilton as the true leader of the Federalists. Together, they attempted to undermine Adams's efforts to negotiate peace with France. By September 30, 1800, however, Adams's negotiators signed an agreement with Napoléon Bonaparte, France's new ruler and self-proclaimed emperor, ending the Quasi-War.

Now, Hamilton went to work spreading false gossip about Adams to make sure that Adams would lose the presidential election of 1800. Hamilton wrote a pamphlet calling Adams a liar and an ungrateful person, unfit for the office of president. A copy of the pamphlet fell into the hands of Republican senator Aaron Burr, who released it to the newspapers.

Adams knew that signing the Alien and Sedition Acts had been a mistake. Indeed, he regarded it as the biggest political blunder of his life. But he took pride in keeping America out of a full-scale war with France, no matter how great the political price. He believed his peace missions to France were his finest achievement. Later, he would write the words he wanted inscribed on his gravestone: "Here lies

John Adams, who took upon himself the responsibility of the peace with France in the year 1800."[3]

New Temporary Home

In June 1800, Adams traveled to Washington, D.C., to inspect the brand new White House, then known as the President's House. Abigail joined him there in November. Only six rooms of the enormous house were ready for occupancy. Abigail wrote, "Surrounded by forests, can you believe that wood is not to be had, because people cannot be found to cut and cart it! . . . We have, indeed, come into a new country."[4]

By the end of the year, the Adamses had become comfortable in their new home. They celebrated Christmas in the White House with a fine feast. However, they still grieved over the death of their son Charles, who had succumbed to illness on December 1. Sadly, this would be their only Christmas in the White House. Adams had lost the election of 1800 to Jefferson, who would become the nation's third president. On January 1, 1801, the Adamses hosted the first White House New Year's Day reception. They would only spend two more months in the White House.

When Abigail Adams first saw the ▷ *"President's House," which was the name at the time for the White House, she felt as if she had come into "a new country." Only six rooms in the house were ready to be occupied, and the building itself was surrounded by forests.*

Chapter 6

Retirement Years at Quincy, 1801–1826

On March 4, 1801, Thomas Jefferson was inaugurated as president. Aaron Burr became vice president. One person was conspicuously absent that day—a bitter John Adams. Early that morning, Adams had climbed into his coach and slipped out of Washington. He was now well on his way back to Braintree, Massachusetts. Adams looked forward to the pleasures of tending to his farm and fields.

Reflecting on his administration, Adams wrote that he had left the nation with "its coffers [treasury] full, and the fair prospects of a peace with all the world smiling in its face, its commerce flourishing, its navy glorious, its agriculture uncommonly productive and lucrative."[1]

During his last days in office, Adams had grown apprehensive about the coming Republican administration. So he nominated Federalists to judicial positions, including John Marshall as chief justice of the United States. The Senate approved the nominations without debate. This greatly angered Jefferson, causing yet more bitterness between the two former friends. Jefferson, in an 1804 letter to Abigail Adams, wrote, "I did consider his last appointments to office as personally unkind. They were from among my most ardent political enemies."[2]

▶ Peacefield

Back in Braintree (which was now named Quincy, after Abigail's grandfather), sixty-five-year-old Adams began his life in retirement. It would be a long, quiet period out of the public eye that would last for just over a quarter of a century. The Adamses renamed their home in Quincy "Peacefield," after the peace Adams had made with France. Life was good. On Sundays, the Adamses would entertain neighbors, friends, and family members who would gather at their home after church.

Adams devoted many hours to reading as well as to writing and reflecting about his political accomplishments. He also spent much of his time writing about the life, times, and ideas of the notable political figures he had known. He constantly wrote letters to his friends in which he further developed his own political philosophy.

▷ Renewed Friendship

In 1812, Adams, at the urging of Dr. Benjamin Rush, finally wrote a letter to his old friend Jefferson, saying that the two of them should not die before explaining themselves to each other. Dr. Rush was a friend of both former presidents. He had told Adams that he had had a dream in which both men began a correspondence that would continue until they "sunk into the grave nearly at the same time."[3] Rush's dream would prove prophetic. Adams and Jefferson did indeed begin a correspondence that would last the rest of their lives. They discussed political matters and questions of science and religion, as well as personal matters, such as the death of Jefferson's daughter Polly. Before long, the two men had reestablished a warm friendship.

On October 18, 1818, Abigail died of typhoid fever. Adams was filled with grief at the loss of his beloved wife, his closest companion, whose constant love and support had sustained him. Jefferson sent Adams his condolences. Adams wrote back, "Your letter of Nov. 13 gave me great delight not only by the divine consolation it afforded me

under my great affliction: but as it gave me full proof of your restoration to health."[4]

▶ Proud Father

Six years later, in 1824, Adams was thrilled when his son John Quincy Adams was elected the sixth president of the United States. John Quincy had followed in his father's footsteps, graduating from Harvard College, becoming a lawyer, then rising through the diplomatic ranks, eventually becoming a U.S. senator, a secretary of state in the administration of President James Monroe, and ultimately president.

On July 4, 1826, the fiftieth anniversary of the Declaration of Independence, ninety-year-old John Adams lay in bed, ill. Early in the afternoon, he roused himself and spoke the words "Thomas Jefferson survives."[5] These were to be Adams's last words. He soon lapsed into a coma and died within several hours. By an amazing coincidence, Jefferson had died that very morning, a few hours before Adams. Eulogies across the nation praised the extraordinary contributions of both Jefferson and Adams, friends and founding fathers.

▶ Legacy

One of Adams's greatest contributions as president was the peaceful transfer of power following the election of 1800. Because Adams was the first president to lose an election,

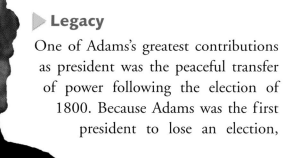

This painting shows John Adams at eighty-eight years of age. Soon, his son John Quincy would be elected the sixth president of the United States.

there was fear that government might be disrupted if Adams refused to resign. But Adams accepted the election's outcome and left office peacefully. That set a precedent and was further proof that the U.S. Constitution worked, since it set the terms for the transfer of power from one president to the next.

The appointment of John Marshall as chief justice of the United States was also part of Adams's legacy as president. Marshall's strength helped the judicial branch of the government to become just as strong as the executive and legislative branches.

Perhaps Adams's greatest achievement as president was in guiding the young country through perilous times, helping the fledgling nation to find its way. Adams was ever mindful of his responsibility to those who would come after him. His sense of needing to lay the right groundwork is clear in the words he wrote in a letter to Abigail on May 12, 1780: "I must study politics and war [so] that my sons may have liberty to study mathematics and philosophy. My sons ought to study mathematics and philosophy, geography, natural history, naval architecture, navigation, commerce, and agriculture in order to give their children a right to study painting, poetry, music, architecture, statuary, tapestry, and porcelain."[6]

Chapter 1. A Sea Adventure, 1778

1. James Bishop Peabody, ed., *The Founding Fathers: John Adams, Biography in His Own Words* (New York: Newsweek, Inc., 1973), p. 214.

2. Ibid., p. 216.

Chapter 2. Early Years, 1735–1758

1. Page Smith, *John Adams: Volume I 1735–1784* (Garden City, N.Y.: Doubleday & Company, Inc., 1962), p. 12.

2. Ibid.

Chapter 3. Lawyer and Revolutionary, 1758–1777

1. Page Smith, *John Adams: Volume I 1735–1784* (Garden City, N.Y.: Doubleday & Company, Inc., 1962), p. 55.

Chapter 4. Diplomat and Vice President, 1777–1797

1. Jack Shepherd, *The Adams Chronicles: Four Generations of Greatness* (Boston: Little, Brown & Company, 1975), p. 92.

2. Ibid., p. 114.

3. Ibid., p. 159.

4. Ibid., p. 157.

Chapter 5. America's Second President, 1797–1801

1. Margaret L. Coit, *The Life History of the United States, Volume 3: 1789–1829, The Growing Years* (New York: Time-Life Books, 1963), p. 35.

2. Ibid.

3. Ibid., p. 36.

4. Jack Shepherd, *The Adams Chronicles: Four Generations of Greatness* (Boston: Little, Brown & Company, 1975), pp. 210, 212.

Chapter 6. Retirement Years at Quincy, 1801–1826

1. Jack Shepherd, *The Adams Chronicles: Four Generations of Greatness* (Boston: Little, Brown & Company, 1975), p. 214.

2. Ibid., pp. 213–214.

3. Ibid., p. 254.

4. James Bishop Peabody, ed., *The Founding Fathers: John Adams, Biography in His Own Words* (New York: Newsweek, Inc., 1973), p. 404.

5. Ibid., p. 407.

6. L. H. Butterfield, ed., *Adams Family Correspondence* (Cambridge, Mass.: Harvard University Press, 1963), vol. 3, p. 342.

Further Reading

Bober, Natalie S. *Abigail Adams: Witness to a Revolution.* New York: Atheneum Books for Young Readers, 1995.

Brill, Marlene Targ. *John Adams: Second President of the United States.* Chicago: Children's Press, 1986.

Burgan, Michael. *John Adams.* Broomall, Pa.: Chelsea House Publishers, 2000.

Kent, Deborah. *The American Revolution: "Give Me Liberty or Give Me Death."* Berkeley Heights, N.J.: Enslow Publishers, Inc., 2000.

McCullough, David. *John Adams.* New York: Simon & Schuster Trade, 2001.

Santrey, Laurence. *John Adams: Brave Patriot.* Mahwah, N.J.: Troll Communications, 1997.

Stefoff, Rebecca. *John Adams: 2nd President of the United States.* Ada, Okla.: Garrett Educational Corporation, 1988.

Weber, Michael. *Washington, Adams, & Jefferson.* Vero Beach, Fla.: Rourke Corporation, 1996.

Welsbacher, Anne. *John Adams.* Minneapolis, Minn.: ABDO Publishing Company, 1998.

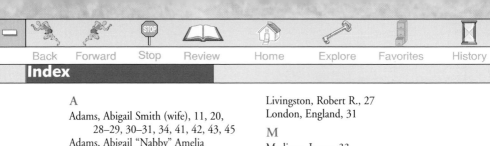